Dear Friends,

It has been a very busy year since the first publication of this book. I am overwhelmed by the tremendous response from the readers. It was a culmination of 4 years work (experimenting and writing and rewriting text) so as to demystify Indian cooking, and to make the recipes simple, healthy and more relevant to todays' Australian. As we enter the new millennium, I have realised that people have become more and more health conscious and want to take an active part in maintaining their own and their families health by choosing balanced and nutritious diet.

Recipes in this book are carefully chosen so as to represent a combination of very healthy ingredients cooked in spices that aid digestion, and very simple cooking techniques. Minimal presence of fats (oil etc) in daily food is the essence of a healthy diet and I have followed this principle in all my recipes making this book rather unique. In short, this book is written to promote healthy ways of cooking tasty Indian food while being sensitive to both time restrictions and your finances.

As "Indian Cuisine Down Under" goes into its second print, I want to share with you some new and exciting developments in the availability of tantalising Indian pastes and ready to use sauces made by "SHARWOODS". Importantly these are now manufactured in South Australia using the most healthy Australian ingredients wherever possible. The range is just fantastic and can be used across all the recipes in this book.

I present to you a collection of my own recipes. They can be used for everyday dining or to create an impressive three course meal when entertaining. I have adapted these recipes to suit the Australian kitchen without loosing the authenticity of the Indian taste or flavour. I am sure that my easy to follow step-by-step instructions and illustrations will guide the most inexperienced cook to achieve perfect & delicious results with ease. I have explored mouth watering vegetarian dishes to tempt the Vegan cooks using very easily available ingredients. There are special hints for weight watchers and for cooking ahead. So enjoy preparing these exotic spicy tastes in your own kitchen to share with your family and friends.

Asha Katdare

INDIAN CUISINE

DOWN UNDER

Author and Editor
DR ASHA KATDARE

Consultant Editor
PENNY ROCHOW

Advertising by
SAR KATDARE LLM

Project Co-Ordinator
MELANIE PARKER

Cover design by
SCOTT DIGITAL (SA)

Cover Photography by
NORMAN WEEDALL
Gainsborough Studio

Printed in Australia by
CUSTOM PRESS
Brompton, SA

First printed 1998
second printing 2000

Published by
Suhas Pty Ltd

All Correspondence to
Indian Cuisine Down Under
PO Box 437 Prospect
South Australia 5082

FOREWORD

In my own cookbook published 20 years ago I said “let me sound off about Australian curry. What seems to be accepted kitchen practice in this country is that curry is a weak stew of meat, sometimes with vegetables or even fruit added to it, and flavoured with two teaspoons of a commercial curry powder. Having at an early age been fed with delicious goat and chicken curries at the table of my father’s great friend Battan Singh, I carefully avoid these Australian insults to a great cuisine.”

That sort of thing still does happen in Australia, though thank goodness there has been great progress to better knowledge. One still, however, finds some cookbooks sold here, (usually those from America or Europe,) where an otherwise well reputed chef will specify in a recipe one or two teaspoons of curry powder without specifying the making of that curry powder (i.e. what spices and in what proportions) so that in fact anyone using the recipe might well produce very different tastes from those appropriate to the dish. For the spices used in Indian cuisine are many and the tastes through the subtle combinations of the spices myriad.

Australians are coming to love the delights of the Indian cuisine, but because of the effort involved in the preparation of many Indian dishes do so only in restaurants. Dr Katdare, realising the problem for two-income families of spending great time and effort in the kitchen has written a book which both promotes healthy Indian food, and solves many of the problems of time and effort to allow the two-income family to enjoy their own home cooking of delicious and authentic dishes.

One of the ways she does this is to advocate the use of commercial curry pastes but she specifies particular curry pastes for particular dishes. i.e. instead of the use of a nondescript curry powder she points out that there is now a great range of prepared ingredients available at shops selling Asian groceries, and within that range it is possible to find the appropriate tastes one looks for in particular dishes. So in each dish described here the tastes wanted are clearly defined – and easily produced.

Australia has long lacked a good and simple book on the cuisine of our Indian heritage written for our present-day society and making available the knowledge of how within the capacity of those who like to cook at home even when leading desperately busy lives, they can accomplish the mouth-watering food which she describes. This is a really *useful* book for the Australian kitchen.

Don Dunstan

CONTENTS

STARTERS

With 14 main languages and 49 major dialects, each region in India is vastly different from each other and this is directly reflected in the foods Indians eat. I have selected a great variety, from the Tandoor dishes of the meat eating north to the mouth watering variation of Masala Dosa (thin crepes) of the south to tempt your palate. All the recipes serve 4 people.

Clockwise from left: Murg Tikka (Tandoori & Hara), Sabzi Kabab, Haddi Kabab, Ghavan Kheema

VEGETARIAN STARTERS

Far from being boring and tasteless, Indian vegetarian starters are very zesty, inexpensive and easy to prepare. They can be used as snacks or to serve as a light luncheon.

PYAS KARANJEE

(Pastry crescents stuffed with spicy onions and capsicum)

Coming home from school was a very special time for my sisters and I, as my mother loved to surprise us with mouthwatering snacks. Karanjee with spicy fillings were one of our favourites.

1 tablespoon safflower oil
1 large onion, finely chopped
1 medium green capsicum, seeded and finely chopped
1/4 teaspoon turmeric
1/4 teaspoon salt
1/4 teaspoon sugar
1/4 teaspoon chilli powder
1 teaspoon lemon juice
2 tablespoons split pea flour (see page 40)
1/4 cup chopped fresh coriander
2 sheets of pampas puff pastry (25cmx25cm)
milk or cream to glaze
coconut coriander chutney, to serve (see page 33)

Heat oil in pan over medium heat, saute onion until golden brown. Add capsicum, turmeric, salt, sugar, chilli, lemon juice, stir well, cover, cook on low for 2 mins. Sprinkle mixture with split pea flour, mix to combine, cover, cook on low for 1 minute. Adjust salt, chilli to taste. Add coriander, set aside to cool. On lightly floured board, roll out pastry sheet to 35cmx35cm (approx 3 mm thick).
Cut 4 rounds with 8-9cm scone cutter - step 1
Use 2 teaspoons filling to make karanjee - step 2
Use pastry cutter to make crescent shapes as in picture - step 3 & 4
Place karanjee on tray lined with baking paper, brush with cream or milk, bake at 250°C until golden brown (approx 10 mins). Serve hot with coconut coriander chutney.

To cook ahead: Prepare filling 24-48 hours ahead and refrigerate. Fill pastry 8-10 hours ahead (brush with milk or cream just prior to baking), dust with flour and separate with plastic wrap to prevent them sticking together. Refrigerate in airtight container. Bake just before serving. Not suitable for freezing

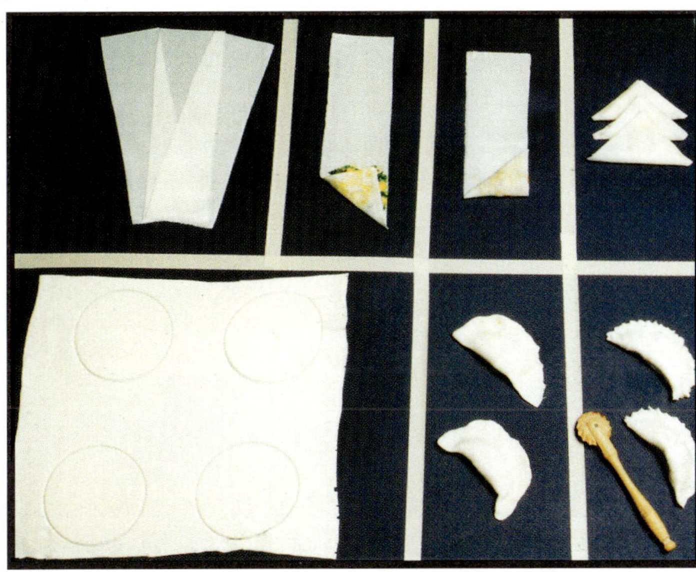

Making Samosa & Pyas Karanjee

SAMOSA

(Pastry triangles with vegetable filling)

1 teaspoon safflower oil
1 cup frozen mixed vegetables
1 small potato, finely chopped
1 teaspoon Sharwood curry paste
1/4 teaspoon chilli powder
1/2 teaspoon salt
1 tablespoon water
4 sheets of spring roll pastry (215mmx215mm)
paste made with cornflour and little water
1/4 cup safflower oil to fry
coconut coriander chutney, to serve (see page 33)

Heat 1 teaspoon oil in pan over medium heat, add mixed vegetables, potato, paste, chilli, salt, water, stir, cover, cook on low until potato is tender (approx 5 mins). Increase heat to cook off excess water, adjust salt, chilli to taste, set aside to cool. Cut each pastry into 3 equal strips. Place 1 heaped spoon of filling at bottom of strip, fold and make 12 triangular samosas as shown in picture below. Seal edges with cornflour paste.
Heat oil in fry pan over medium heat. Fry samosas until golden brown on both sides. Drain on absorbent paper. Serve hot with coconut coriander chutney.

To cook ahead: Prepare 24-48 hours ahead, refrigerate in airtight container. Deep-fry samosas 4-6 hours ahead and reheat in oven at 120°C for 30 mins. Not suitable for freezing.

MASALA GHAVAN

(crepe with spicy potato & onion filling)

The filling in this preparation is very much like the filling in the traditional south Indian masala dosa (a large crisp crepe made from rice and lentil flour).

For ghavan
2 eggs
pinch of salt
1 cup milk
1/2 cup plain flour
2 teaspoon safflower oil
olive oil spray
For filling
1 tablespoon safflower oil
1/2 teaspoon brown mustard seeds (see page 40)
1 medium onion, thinly sliced
1/2 teaspoon turmeric
1/2 teaspoon chilli powder or 1 small chilli, chopped
2 large potatoes, thinly sliced
1tablespoon lemon juice
1/2 teaspoon salt
1/2 teaspoon sugar
1/4 cup chopped fresh coriander
coconut coriander chutney, to serve (see page 33)

For ghavan, combine eggs, salt, milk using beater. Slowly add flour, oil to make smooth batter. Refrigerate for1 hour.
Heat nonstick fry pan, spray with olive oil, make 10 thin crepes (approx. 12 1/2cm in diameter). Stack, keep warm.
For filling, heat oil in nonstick pan over medium heat, add mustard seeds, as they pop, add onion, saute until light brown. Add turmeric, chilli, potato, lemon juice, salt, sugar, stir , cover, cook on low, (stir occasionally) until potato is tender (approx 15 mins). Adjust salt, chilli to taste, add coriander. Spoon filling into centre of crepe, fold over. Serve hot with coconut coriander chutney.
To cook ahead: Prepare crepes and filling 24-48 hours ahead and refrigerate separately. Warm separately in oven at 150°C for 30 mins.
Weightwatchers leave out oil in batter and use low-fat milk.

SABZI KABAB

(mixed vegetable patties)

2 tablespoons safflower oil
1 tablespoon Sharwood curry paste
1cup frozen mixed vegetables
2 large potatoes, boiled, peeled and mashed
1/2 teaspoon salt
1 teaspoon lemon juice
1/4 teaspoon sugar
1/2 teaspoon chilli powder (optional)
1/4 cup chopped fresh coriander
1 beaten egg, breadcrumbs for coating
coconut coriander chutney, to serve (see page 33)

Heat 1 teaspoon oil in pan, add curry paste, frozen vegetables, cover, cook on low until vegetables are tender (approx), let it cool. Combine rest of the ingredients with cooked vegetables, adjust salt to taste. Shape into 10 patties. Dip in egg and coat with breadcrumbs. Heat remaining oil in nonstick fry pan over medium to low heat, brown patties on both sides. Drain on absorbent paper. Serve hot with coconut coriander chutney.
To cook ahead: Prepare patties 24-48 hours ahead, refrigerate in air tight container. Cook 4-6 hours ahead and reheat, uncovered, in 150 °C oven on foil-lined tray for 30 mins. Not suitable for freezing.

BATATA WADA

(potato balls in spicy lentil batter)

This savoury snack from Bombay is a great favourite of university students. It is nutritionally sound and easy on your pocket.

For wada
2 large potatoes, half boiled and grated
1 small onion, finely chopped
1/2 teaspoon minced garlic
1/2 teaspoon minced ginger
1/4 cup chopped fresh coriander
1 teaspoon dessicated coconut
1 teaspoon lemon juice
1/2 teaspoon sugar
1 teaspoon salt
For batter
1/4 cup split pea flour (see page 40)
1/4 teaspoon turmeric (see page 40)
1/4 teaspoon salt
1/4 teaspoon chilli powder
pinch of bicarbonate of soda (optional)
1/3 cup water (approx)
1/3 cup safflower oil, for deep frying
coconut coriander chutney, to serve(see page 33)

To make wada mix all ingredients, adjust salt, chilli to taste. Shape into 12 flat rounds. Refrigerate for 1 hour to firm.
To make batter mix all ingredients (except water), add water to make thick batter.
Heat oil in small pan over medium heat. Dip wada in batter, slip into oil few at a time, fry on both sides until golden brown. Drain on absorbent paper.
Serve hot with coconut coriander chutney.
To cook ahead: Prepare wada 24-48 hours ahead and refrigerate. Fry 4-6 hours ahead and reheat, uncovered, in 120°C oven for 30 mins. Not suitable for freezing.

NON-VEGETARIAN STARTERS

Australia's cold winters provide the perfect backdrop for preparing Indian recipes. When summer arrives and Australians move outdoors, these same recipes can be prepared on your backyard barbecue.

Clockwise from left: Karanjee, Batata Wada, Machi Kabab, Samosa, Masala Ghavan, Seekh Kabab

MACHI KABAB

(fish patties)

My mother always managed to turn leftover fish into mouthwatering fish patties with her innovative use of spices.

2 large potatoes, boiled, mashed
1 cup cooked boneless fish
***OR** 185g can tuna in brine, drained.*
1 teaspoon minced ginger
1 teaspoon minced garlic
1/2 teaspoon chilli powder
1/2 teaspoon salt
1/4 cup chopped fresh coriander
1 egg, beaten
breadcrumbs to coat
2 tablespoons safflower oil
coconut garlic chutney, to serve (see page 33)

Combine potato, fish, ginger, garlic, salt, chilli, coriander. Adjust salt, chilli to taste. Shape into 10 oval patties. Dip in egg, coat with breadcrumbs, place in refrigerator for 1 hour.

Heat oil in nonstick fry pan over medium heat, brown patties on both sides. Serve hot with coconut garlic chutney.

To cook ahead: Prepare patties 24-48 hours ahead and refrigerate in airtight container. Brown patties 4-6 hours ahead. Reheat, uncovered, in oven at 150°C for 20 mins. Not suitable for freezing.

SEEKH KABAB

(mince on skewers)

This quick and easy recipe almost always promises to leave a magical taste on the tongue of your family and friends.

250gm lean chicken or beef or pork mince
1/2 onion, finely chopped
2 teaspoons Sharwood tandoori paste
1 teaspoon minced ginger
1 teaspoon minced garlic
1 teaspoon salt
1/4 teaspoon chilli powder
2 teaspoons dried fenugreek leaves (optional - see page 40)
1 tablespoon breadcrumbs
1/4 cup chopped fresh coriander
1 egg, beaten
10 wooden skewers
coconut garlic chutney, to serve (see page 33)

Mix all ingredients until well combined. Adjust salt, chilli to taste, refrigerate for 1 hour to bind meat. Divide mixture into 10 portions and, with wet hands, shape around skewers to make sausages. Grill on both sides until golden brown and meat is cooked through. Serve hot with coconut garlic chutney.
To cook ahead: Shape seekh kababs 4-6 hours ahead and refrigerate. Alternatively, prepare mince mixture in advance and freeze for 4-6 weeks. Thaw in refrigerator, shape onto skewers and cook as directed, just before serving. Great for barbecue.

GHAVAN KHEEMA

(Crepe with spicy mince, peas & potato filling)

When my sons were at school, saturday morning lunch was a very special time in our household. After the school sport, my sons and their friends would descend on our kitchen table and hold contests to see who could eat the most, Ghavan Kheema being their most favourite.

For filling:
1 tablespoon safflower oil
1 small onion, finely chopped
400 gms lean chicken or beef or pork mince
1 tablespoon Sharwood Tikka masala paste
1/2 teaspoon salt
1/2 teaspoon chilli powder
1/2 cup frozen peas
1 small potato, finely chopped
3 tablespoons water
coconut coriander chutney, to serve (see page 33)

To make Ghavan:
see page 6
To make filling, heat oil in pan over medium heat, saute onion until transparent. Add mince, masala paste, salt, chilli, stir until the meat is separated and cooked through. Add peas, potato, water, cover, cook on low until potato is tender (approx 8 mins). Increase heat to cook off excess water. Adjust salt, chilli to taste. Spoon filling into the centre of each crepe, roll up. Serve hot with coconut coriander chutney.
To cook ahead: Prepare crepes and filling 24-48 hrs ahead and refrigerate separately. Warm separately in oven at 150°C for 30 mins. Crepes are suitable for freezing. Filling suitable for freezing if potato is not used.

HADDI KABAB

(baked lamb cutlets in spicy tandoori sauce)

Succulent marinated meat cooked by dry heat was a speciality of mughal times and in present times is a culinary delight eaten by all meat lovers.
8-10 french lamb cutlets
1 cup natural yogurt
2 tablespoons Sharwood tandoori paste
1 teaspoon salt
mint chutney, to serve (see page 34)

Stab cutlets with fork few times (this allows marinade to penetrate). Combine yogurt, tandoori paste, salt, add cutlets, toss to coat well. Refrigerate for 12-24 hours. Place cutlets on foil-lined oven tray, spoon 1 teaspoon of marinade on each cutlet, brown on both sides under hot grill. Cover tray with foil, bake for 20 mins in preheated oven at 200°C. Uncover, bake for 10 mins longer. Serve hot with mint chutney.
To cook ahead: Freeze cutlets in marinade, thaw in refrigerator and bake as directed. Freeze baked cutlets and reheat, covered in 150°C oven for 45 mins although this may dull its red colour. Great to barbecue. For really spicy hot cutlets, add 1extra tablespoon of tandoori paste and 1/2 teaspoon of chilli powder to marinade.

MURG TIKKA

(marinated chicken on skewers)

Hara (marinated in green spicy herbs paste)
Tandoori (marinated in traditional tandoori paste)

500gms of boneless chicken
For Hara Marinade
1 teaspoon salt
1 tablespoon natural yogurt
1/4 cup chopped fresh mint
*1/2 teaspoon chilli powder **OR** 1 fresh green chilli*
2 teaspoons minced ginger
2 teaspoons minced garlic
For Tandoori Marinade
1 cup natural yogurt
2 tablespoons Sharwood tandoori paste
1 teaspoon salt
mint chutney, to serve (see page 34)

Remove skin from chicken, trim excess fat, cut into 5 cm cubes. Keep aside.
To make hara marinade mix all ingredients in blender until smooth.
To make tandoori marinade combine all ingredients in bowl.
Add chicken to marinade, toss to coat well, refrigerate for 12-24 hours. Thread chicken pieces on skewers, place on foil-lined oven tray, cook under preheated hot grill, rotating twice and chicken is cooked through (approx 15 mins). Serve hot with mint chutney.
To cook ahead: Marinate chicken, thread onto skewers and freeze upto 4-6 weeks. Thaw in refrigerator, cook as directed. Great to barbecue.

Weightwatchers use low-fat yogurt.

SAUCES

YOGURT SAUCE

1 cup natural yogurt
1/4 teaspoon cumin powder
1/4 teaspoon sugar
1/2 teaspoon salt

Mix yogurt with cumin, sugar, salt in serving bowl and refrigerate.

CREAMY CHILLI SAUCE

1 tablespoon safflower oil
1 medium onion, finely chopped
1 teaspoon minced ginger
1 teaspoon minced garlic
1/4 cup cooked, mashed pumpkin
1 teaspoon Sharwood Tikka masala paste (mixed with 2 teaspoons paprika)
1/4 teaspoon salt
1/4 teaspoon chilli powder (optional)
1/4 cup chopped red capsicum
1/4 cup sour light cream
1/4 cup chopped fresh coriander

Heat oil in small pan, saute onion, garlic, ginger until golden brown. Add pumpkin, masala paste, salt, chilli powder(if using), stir for 1 min, add capsicum, cover and cook on low for 1 minute, add water, bring to boil, stir till thick paste is formed. Adjust salt, chilli to taste. Remove from heat, stir in cream, coriander. Serve hot.

CREAMY CURRY SAUCE

1 tablespoon safflower oil
1 small onion, finely chopped
2 cloves garlic, chopped
1 teaspoon garam masala (see page 40)
1 teaspoon Sharwood curry paste
1/4 teaspoon salt
1/4 teaspoon chilli powder
1/4 cup chopped mushroom
1/4 cup water
1/4 cup chopped fresh coriander
1/4 cup cream

Heat oil in small pan, saute onion, garlic until golden brown. Add garam masala, curry paste, salt, chilli, stir for 1 min, add mushrooms, cover, cook for 1 min, add water, bring to boil, stir till thick paste is formed. Adjust salt, chilli to taste, stir in coriander cream. Serve hot

COCONUT SAUCE

1/2 cup dessicated coconut
3 cloves
1 cup water

Dry roast coconut in a nonstick fry pan until golden brown. Set aside to cool. In dry grinder grind coconut, clove to fine powder, transfer to blender, add water and blend to thin paste.
To cook ahead: Prepare ahead. Freeze upto 4-6 weeks.

MAIN COURSES

Believe it or not there is no such thing as curry in India. There is always a curried version (with thick or more liquid gravy) of main dish in every meal. This can be made from vegetables, meat (usually chicken, goat or lamb) or fish. The rest of the menu is chosen to compliment the main dish and to represent a very balanced diet. I have presented all these from the creamy, spicy meat preparations of the north to the more simple and wholesome curried lentils of the south, to the mouthwatering seafood preparations of the coastal regions. All the recipes serve 4 people.

Clockwise from left: Sabzi Damayanti, Daal Methi, Murg Sagwala

VEGETARIAN MAIN COURSES

With the choice of innumerable lentils and vegetables, Indian vegetarian cooking is very sophisticated and original.

SABZI DAMAYANTI

(mixed vegetables in cream sauce)

My paternal grandmother always insisted that the secret of maintaining good health was a well planned meal which included plenty of fresh vegetables cooked in herbs and spices.

2 tablespoons natural yogurt
1/2 teaspoon salt
2 teaspoon Sharwood curry paste
1 teaspoon sugar
1 medium eggplant (optional), cut in 5 cm cubes
200g cauliflower floret (4 cm heads) with stems
2 tablespoons safflower oil
1/2 teaspoon cumin seeds
1 large potato, peeled, cut lengthwise 1/2 cm thick
1 medium red capsicum seeded, thinly sliced
1/2 cup drained canned kidney beans ***OR*** *1/2 cup cooked chickpeas*
1/2 teaspoon chilli powder
1/2 cup mushrooms
150g snow peas cut in half
1 tablespoon thickened light cream
chopped fresh coriander, to garnish

Combine yogurt, salt, curry paste, sugar in bowl, add eggplant, cauliflower, toss to coat, marinate for 1 hour.
Heat oil in pan on medium heat, add cumin seeds as they turn black, add potato, cover, cook on high for 1 minute. Add eggplant, cauliflower (save marinade), cook on high for 1 minute. Cover, cook on low for 4 mins, stir once. Add capsicum, kidney beans or chickpeas, reserved marinade, chilli, stir on high for 1 minute. Add mushrooms, snow peas, cover, cook on low for 1 minute. Add cream just before serving. Serve hot garnished with fresh coriander.
To cook ahead: Prepare 24-48 hours ahead, refrigerate. For best results, reheat in pan over high heat, stirring constantly. Not suitable for freezing.

DAAL METHI

(curried lentils with fenugreek and spinach)

1 cup red lentils (see page 40)
1/2 cup split peas (see page 40)
2 tablespoons safflower oil
1/4 teaspoon fenugreek seeds (see page 40)
2 cloves garlic, chopped
1 small onion, finely chopped
1/4 teaspoon turmeric
1/2 teaspoon chilli powder
3 cups water
1 cup cooked spinach
OR *150g frozen spinach*
1/2 teaspoon sugar
2 teaspoons salt
1 tablespoon lemon juice
chopped fresh coriander, to garnish

Soak lentils, split pea in water overnight, drain, set aside. Heat oil in pan, add fenugreek seeds, garlic, saute until golden brown. Add onion, saute until transparent. Add lentils, turmeric, chilli, cook on high for 1 minute. Add water, bring to boil, cover, simmer on low, stir occasionally, until lentils are tender (approx 12-15 mins). Stir in spinach, sugar, salt, lemon juice, bring to boil, cook for 2 mins. Adjust salt, chilli to taste. Serve hot garnished with fresh coriander.
To cook ahead: Prepare ahead, freeze for up to 4-6 weeks before using.

GOBI MAKA

(cabbage with corn)

1 tablespoon safflower oil
1/4 teaspoon brown mustard seeds (see page 40)
3 cups diced cabbage
1/2 cup frozen corn
1/4 teaspoon turmeric
1/4 teaspoon chilli powder
1/2 teaspoon salt
1 teaspoon lemon juice
1/4 teaspoon sugar
chopped fresh coriander, to garnish

Heat oil in pan, add mustard seeds, as they pop, add cabbage, corn and remaining ingredients. Cover, cook on low, until cabbage is cooked (approx 4-5mins), stir occasionally. Adjust salt, chilli to taste. Serve hot garnished with fresh coriander.

To cook ahead: Prepare 24-48 hours ahead, refrigerate. For best results, reheat in pan over high heat, stirring constantly. Not suitable for freezing.

RAJMA

(red kidney beans in spicy sauce)

2 tablespoons safflower oil
1/2 teaspoon cumin seeds
1 medium onion, finely chopped
1 teaspoon Sharwood Tikka masala paste
1/2 teaspoon garam masala (see page 40)
1x440g can red kidney beans
1/2 teaspoon salt
1/2 cup water
1 tablespoon thickened light cream
chopped fresh coriander, to garnish

Heat oil in pan, add cumin seeds, as they turn black add onion, saute until golden brown. Add masala paste, garam masala, cook for 1 minute. Add red kidney beans, salt, cook on high for 1 minute. Add water, bring to boil. Reduce heat, cover, cook on low for 2-3 mins, stir once. Adjust salt to taste, add cream before serving. Serve hot garnished with fresh coriander.

To cook ahead: Prepare ahead, freeze (without cream) upto 4-6 weeks before using. Stir in cream just before serving.

Weightwatchers substitute low fat evaporated milk for cream.

Gobi Maka & Rajma

CHOLE

(chickpeas in garlic sauce)

Fibre in our daily diet plays an important role in maintaining good health. Chickpeas (legumes) are high in fibre. My sons love "chole & bhatoore" (fried indian bread) and I am sure your family would find it delicious too.

1 1/2 cups chickpeas
***OR** 2x440g can cooked chickpeas*
3 tablespoons safflower oil
2 medium onions, finely chopped
3 teaspoons minced garlic
1/2 teaspoon turmeric
1/2 teaspoon chilli powder
3 teaspoons coriander powder
3 teaspoons cumin powder
2 teaspoons garam masala (see page 40)
1 1/2 teaspoon salt
1 cup water
3 cloves garlic, chopped
1 tablespoon thickened light cream
chopped fresh coriander, to garnish

Soak uncooked chickpeas overnight in hot water, drain (to avoid flatulence associated with lentils and beans, it is important to drain lentils and chickpeas after soaking), cook in large pan of simmering water for 20 mins or until tender (use pressure cooker, if you prefer, to speed up this step). Drain , set aside.
Heat oil in pan over medium heat, saute onion, minced garlic until golden brown. Add turmeric, chilli, coriander and cumin powder, garam masala, stir for 1 minute, add chickpeas, salt, water, bring to boil. Reduce heat, cover, cook for 2 mins, uncover, simmer until curry thickens (approx 2 mins). Adjust salt, chilli to taste.
In separate small pan, heat 1 teaspoon oil, saute chopped garlic until golden brown. Stir in cream. Sprinkle over warm chickpeas. Serve hot garnished with coriander.
To cook ahead: Prepare chickpeas, freeze for upto 4-6 weeks before using. Sprinkle cream, garlic to heated chickpeas before serving.
Weightwatchers substitute low-fat evaporated milk for cream.

Chole

DAAL MAHESHWARI

(spicy mixed lentils)

Daals made from lentils represent a major source of protein, complex carbohydrate, minerals and vitamins. This mixed lentil daal is a great favourite of my friends and can be prepared ahead.

*1/4 cup uncooked chickpeas **OR** 1/2 cup cooked chickpeas*
1/4 cup black-eyed beans (see page 40)
1/4 cup red lentils (see page 40)
1/4 cup brown lentils or masura (see page 40)
2 tablespoons safflower oil
1/2 teaspoon cumin seeds
1 small onion, finely chopped
2 teaspoons Sharwood Tikka masala paste
1 teaspoon salt
1 small tomato, finely chopped
1/4 cup cooked red kidney beans
1 tablespoon thickened light cream
chopped fresh coriander, to garnish

Cook chickpeas as stated in the previous recipe (chole). Soak overnight black-eyed beans, lentils in water , drain. Place beans, lentils in 2 cups of boiling water, cover, simmer on low for 15 mins. Set aside.
Heat oil in pan over medium heat, add cumin seeds as they turn black, add onion, saute until golden brown. Add masala paste, salt, tomato, stir for 2 mins. Add lentils, beans with their water, cooked chickpeas, red kidney beans, stir well for 2 mins. Adjust salt, chilli to taste, add cream, just before serving. Serve hot garnished with fresh coriander.
To cook ahead: Prepare daal ahead, freeze for upto 4-6 weeks before using.
Weightwatchers substitute low-fat evaporated milk for cream.

Daal Maheshwari

NONVEGETARIAN MAIN COURSES

Many of the Indian meat preparations have been influenced by the Mughal cuisine as Mughals ruled India for more than 500 years. The meat and poultry that is so plentiful in Australia, undoubtedly is the best in the world and when these are cooked using the flavoursome Indian recipes, the results are unparalleled.

VINDALOO

(Succulent pork or beef in very very hot sauce)
This preparation from the south is not for the faint hearted but for the lovers of chilli hot food it's a heavenly experience.

500gms diced lean beef or pork
1/4 cup natural yogurt
1 teaspoon salt
1/4 cup fresh mint, finely chopped
2 tablespoons safflower oil
1 large onion, finely chopped
2 tablespoons Sharwood vindaloo paste
2 teaspoons garam masala (see page 40)
2 small tomatoes, finely chopped
2 tablespoons cream
chopped fresh coriander to garnish

Mix meat with yogurt, salt, mint and marinate in refrigerator for 2 hours.
Place meat under grill in foil-lined oven tray, brown on both sides (save marinade). This helps to seal the juices. Keep aside.
Heat oil in pan, saute onion until golden brown, add vindaloo paste, garam masala, stir for 2 mins, add tomato, stir till thick paste is formed. Add browned meat with its juices and saved marinade, stir well, cover, cook on low until meat is tender (approx 40 mins for pork and 55 mins for beef), stir occasionally to prevent meat sticking to pan, (you may have to add a little water to make thick gravy). Add cream just before serving. Serve hot garnished with coriander.
To cook ahead: Prepare ahead, freeze (without cream) for up to 4-6 weeks. Thaw in refrigerator. Add cream to heated curry just before serving.
Weightwatchers substitute low-fat evaporated milk for cream.

MURG SAGWALA

(chicken with spinach)
There are numerous varieties of spinach available in India and they are used in combination with red or white meat to impart a rich and unique flavour.

500gm boneless skinned chicken
2 teaspoons minced ginger
2 teaspoons minced garlic
1/4 cup natural yogurt
1teaspoon salt
2 tablespoons safflower oil
1 cinnamon stick
1 large onion, finely chopped
2 tablespoons Sharwood curry paste
125gm frozen spinach, thawed
***OR** 1 cup chopped, cooked, fresh spinach*

Trim excess fat from chicken, cut in 5 cm pieces. Mix ginger, garlic, yogurt, salt, add chicken, toss to coat, marinate in refrigerator for 8-12 hours. Place chicken on foil-lined tray (save marinade), brown chicken on both sides under grill.
Heat oil in medium pan, add cinnamon stick, as it turns black, add onion, saute until golden brown, add curry paste, stir on high for 1 minute, add chicken (save cooking liquid from tray), spinach, stir for 4 mins. Add saved marinade, liquid from cooking tray, stir, cover, cook until chicken is tender (approx 5 mins). Adjust salt to taste. Serve hot garnished with fresh coriander.
To cook ahead: Prepare and freeze up to 4-6 weeks before using. Thaw in refrigerator.

Clockwise from left: Papadam, Khichadi, Pork Vindaloo, Beef Vindaloo

In recent times, it has become very fashionable to serve kangaroo steak in restaurants. With the following recipe you can combine fashion and originality and surprise your guests.Kangaroo meat is a concentrated source of very easily absorbable iron. It is also very high in protein and low in fat or cholesterol. Kangaroo meat has delicious game flavour and is very quick to cook (grill, barbecue or stir-fry). It is sold at a very affordable price. This recipe of panfried kangaroo meat, blends with many types of sauces. This makes it an excellent addition to your menu.

Clockwise from left: Gosh Sahajani, Murg Dahiwala & Kadai Kangaroo

KADAI KANGAROO

(Panfried fillet of kangaroo with creamy chilli sauce)

500gm kangaroo fillet
1 tablespoon whole meal flour (atta)
1 tablespoon semolina
1/2 teaspoon salt
1 tablespoon safflower oil
creamy chilli sauce (see page 9)
OR
creamy curry sauce (see page 9)
1/4 cup chopped fresh coriander

Cut kangaroo fillet into 6cmx4cm pieces, beat it to tenderise. Mix flour, semolina, salt on kitchen paper. Coat each piece well with flour. Heat oil in nonstick fry-pan on low-medium heat, brown meat on both sides. Cook meat for 2-3 mins, turning once. Place meat on serving dish, spoon over with prepared sauce (piping hot). Serve hot garnished with fresh coriander.
To cook ahead: Coat meat for 8-12 hours ahead and refrigerate in sealed container. Prepare sauce of your choice, freeze for upto 4-6 weeks, thaw in refrigerator. Heat and spoon over on cooked meat. Cook meat just before serving. Great to barbecue.

MACHI MAKHANI

(fish in cream sauce)

1 tablespoon safflower oil
1 large onion, finely chopped
2 teaspoons minced garlic
1 tablespoon Sharwood tandoori paste
1 teaspoon tomato paste
1/4 teaspoon salt
1/4 teaspoon chilli powder
1/2 cup natural yogurt
1/4 cup chopped fresh coriander
500g boneless white fish fillets, cut into 2.5cm pieces
1 tablespoon thickened light cream

Heat oil in pan, saute onion until golden brown. Add garlic, saute until golden brown. Add tandoori and tomato paste, salt, chilli, yogurt, stir 2 mins. Remove pan from heat, add coriander, set aside to cool.
Add fish to pan, toss to coat, place pan in the refrigerator for 2 hours. Return pan to heat, cook for 1 minute, cover, cook on low until fish flakes when tested with a fork (approx 2 mins). Adjust salt to taste. Add cream just before serving.
To cook ahead: For really hot spicy dish, add 1/4-1/2 teaspoon of extra chilli powder. Prepare (without cream) 24-48 hours ahead and refrigerate. Not suitable for freezing. Add cream just before serving.
Weightwatchers substitute low-fat evaporated milk for cream.

GOSH SHAHAJANI

(spicy lamb in mint and yogurt sauce)

500g boneless lamb
3 tablespoons safflower oil
1 large onion, finely chopped
2 tablespoons Sharwood Medium Curry paste
1/4 cup chopped fresh mint
1/2 cup chopped fresh coriander
1 1/2 teaspoon cinnamon powder
1/2 teaspoon salt
1/2 teaspoon chilli powder
3 tablespoons natural yogurt
1/4 cup water

Trim excess fat from lamb, cut into 2.5cm cubes. Heat oil in pan over high heat, brown lamb a little at a time. Remove from pan, set aside. Add onion to pan, saute until golden brown. Add curry paste, mint, coriander, cinnamon, salt, chilli, yogurt, stir until thick paste is formed. Add lamb, stir on high for 1 minute, add water, cover, cook on low until lamb is tender (approx 35-40 mins), stir occasionally to prevent sticking (you may have to add a little water to prevent meat sticking to pan). Adjust salt, chilli to taste. Serve hot garnished with fresh coriander.
To cook ahead: Prepare ahead, freeze 4-6 weeks before using.

MURG DAHIWALA

(butter chicken)

Marinating chicken or meat in a spicy yogurt marinade is the basis of cooking succulent and tasty meat or chicken dishes. Marination allows the special blend of spices to penetrate the fibres, giving extra flavour.

500g skinned boneless chicken
1/2 cup natural yogurt
1 teaspoon salt
2 tablespoons Sharwood tandoori paste
2 tablespoons safflower oil
2 medium onions, finely chopped
2 teaspoons minced ginger
2 teaspoons minced garlic
2 teaspoons tomato paste
1 tablespoon cream
chopped fresh coriander, to garnish

Trim excess fat, cut into 3cm pieces. Mix yogurt, salt, tandoori paste, add chicken, toss to coat, marinate in refrigerator for 12-24 hours.
Heat oil in pan, saute onion until golden brown. Add garlic, ginger, saute until golden brown. Add tomato paste, chicken (save marinade), stir on high for 4 mins. Add marinade, stir on high for 2 mins. Cover and simmer on low for 5 mins until chicken is cooked through. Stir in cream. Serve hot garnished with fresh coriander.
To cook ahead: Prepare ahead and freeze for upto 4-6 weeks.
Weightwatchers substitute low-fat evaporated milk for cream.

KHEEMA MATTAR

(deliciously spicy mince with peas)

There is a tale that the mughal emperor Humayun (great great grandfather of emperor Shahajahan, who built Taj Mahal in 1600) lost all his teeth at the age of 40 and hence the royal chef was ordered to prepare meat dishes that the toothless emperor could eat. The innovative royal chef ground the meat and mince curry was born.

2 tablespoons safflower oil
3 cloves
1 inch stick cinnamon
3 whole pepper corns
1 large onion, finely chopped
500gms lean lamb, beef, chicken or pork mince
1 tablespoon garam masala (see page 40)
1 tablespoon coriander powder
1/2 teaspoon chilli powder
1 cup frozen peas
1/2 cup natural yogurt
1 teaspoon salt
***To garnish** 1 boiled egg & 1/4 cup fresh chopped coriander,*

Heat oil in pan, add clove, cinnamon, pepper corn. As clove and pepper corn pop, add onion, saute until transparent, add mince, garam masala, coriander powder, chilli powder, stir till meat is browned and separated. Add yogurt, peas, salt, stir well, cover, cook on low till mince is cooked (approx 5 mins). Adjust salt, chilli to taste. Serve hot garnished with sliced egg and sprinkled with coriander on top.
To cook ahead: Prepare ahead , freeze for 4-6 weeks.

Clockwise from left: Kaju Batata Rassa, Papadam, Kheema Mattar & Machi Makhani

ZINGA KADHI

(garlic prawns in spicy coconut sauce)

500g uncooked prawns, shelled
1 teaspoon salt
1 teaspoon turmeric
1/2 teaspoon tamarind concentrate (see page 40)
1/2 teaspoon chilli powder
1 tablespoon safflower oil
2 cloves garlic, chopped
1 large onion, finely chopped
coconut sauce (see page 9)
chopped fresh coriander, to garnish

Devein prawns, rinse, drain. Add salt, turmeric, tamarind concentrate, chilli, toss to coat, set aside. Heat oil in pan, saute garlic until golden brown, add onion, saute till transparent. Add prawns, stir on high until prawns turn pink (approx 2 mins). Add coconut sauce, bring to boil, simmer for 2 mins. Adjust salt, chilli to taste, remove from heat. Serve hot garnished with fresh coriander.
To cook ahead: Prepare ahead, freeze for 4-6 weeks before using.

Gosh kashimiri

Zinga Kadhi, Mattar Pilav, Keshar Pilav, Gajjar Pilav

GOSH KASHMIRI

(spicy curried lamb with tomato)

500g boneless lamb
1/4 cup safflower oil
2 large onions, finely chopped
2 teaspoons minced ginger
2 teaspoons minced garlic
2 teaspoons coriander powder
3 teaspoons Sharwood Tikka masala paste (mixed with 2 teaspoons paprika)
1/2 teaspoon chilli powder (optional)
2 medium tomatoes, chopped
1/4 cup water
chopped fresh coriander, to garnish

Trim excess fat from lamb, cut into 2.5cm cubes. Heat oil in thick-based pan over high heat, brown lamb, little at a time, on all sides. Remove lamb from pan, set aside.
Add onion to pan, saute until golden brown. Add ginger, garlic, saute until golden brown. Add coriander powder, masala paste, salt, chilli (if using), stir on medium for 1 minute. Add tomato, cover, cook on low for 5 mins, stir occasionally. Add meat, cook on high for 1 minute, add water, cover, cook on low until meat is tender (approx. 35-40 mins), stir occasionally to prevent sticking. Adjust salt and chilli to taste. Serve hot garnished with fresh coriander.
To cook ahead: Prepare ahead and freeze for upto 4-6 weeks before using.

SPECIAL DISHES

Every region in India has its own specialities inspired by race, religion, history and geography. These recipes, too, incorporate my own individual touch, coupled with special tips passed down to me by the women in my family.

Clockwise from top: Uman, Vegetarian Kofta, Dahi Wada

DAHI WADA

(fried lentil balls in tangy yogurt sauce)

This dish is eaten as a snack or an accompaniment to the main meal. Sprinkle with date chutney, before serving.

For Wada

1/2 cup mung daal (see page 40)
1/4 cup udad daal (see page 40)
1/4 teaspoon salt
1/2 teaspoon minced ginger
1/4 cup water
1 tablespoon chopped fresh coriander
1/2 cup safflower oil, for deep-frying
1/4 teaspoon paprika
date chutney to serve (see page 33)

Yogurt Sauce (see page 9)

For wada, soak both daals in water overnight, drain. In blender, combine daals, salt, ginger, water to make very thick paste. In bowl mix lentil paste, coriander. Heat oil in small pan over medium heat. Slip heaped teaspoonful of mixture into oil, deep-fry until golden brown. Drain on absorbent paper. Makes 16 wadas. Soak wadas in hot water for 3 mins, squeeze water out by pressing each wada between palms of your hands, arrange in yogurt sauce. Sprinkle with paprika, refrigerate. Serve cold with date chutney.
To cook ahead: Prepare 24 hours ahead. Not suitable for freezing.

KAJU BATATA RASSA

(curried potato with cashew nuts)

This was a speciality of my maternal grandmother. For a really hot Rassa, add extra cloves and chilli powder.
2 tablespoons safflower oil
1 large onion, finely chopped
1 large potato, peeled, chopped in 6 pieces
1/4 cup cashew nuts
1/4 teaspoon turmeric
1/2 teaspoon chilli powder
1/2 teaspoon salt
coconut sauce (see page 9)
chopped fresh coriander, to garnish

Heat oil in pan, saute onion until golden brown. Add potato, cashew nuts, turmeric, chilli, salt, cover, cook on low until potatoes are cooked. Add coconut liquid, bring to boil and simmer for 1 minute. Adjust salt, chilli to taste, remove from heat. Serve hot garnished with fresh coriander.
To cook ahead: Prepare 24-48 hours ahead, refrigerate. Not suitable for freezing.

UMAN

(fish in tangy coconut sauce)

Fish is an excellent source of protein, vitamins and minerals. This Goan recipe is mouthwatering and easy to prepare.

500g firm, boneless fish fillets cut in 5 cm pieces.
1/2 teaspoon salt
1/2 cup dessicated coconut
1/2 teaspoon chilli powder
1 teaspoon turmeric
1 teaspoon coriander powder
1/2 cup water
1 tablespoon safflower oil
1 medium onion, finely chopped
1 teaspoon tamarind concentrate
chopped fresh coriander, to garnish

Mix fish with salt in bowl, refrigerate. Grind coconut, chilli, turmeric, coriander in dry grinder to very fine powder. Mix coconut powder with water, set aside. Heat oil in pan, saute onion until golden brown. Add tamarind concentrate and fish, stir gently on medium heat for 1 minute, add coconut liquid , bring to boil, simmer for 1 minute, remove from heat, adjust salt, chilli to taste. Serve hot garnished with fresh coriander, accompanied by boiled rice.
To cook ahead:Prepare fish curry 24-48 hours ahead, refrigerate. Not suitable for freezing.

VEGETABLE KOFTA

(spiced curry with fried cheese balls)

For curry:
1 tablespoon safflower oil
1 large onion, finely chopped
1 teaspoon minced ginger
1 teaspoon minced garlic
2 teaspoons Sharwood Tikka masala paste (mixed with 2 teaspoons paprika)
2 teaspoons fennel powder
1 large tomato, finely chopped
1 tablespoon crushed almonds
1 cup water
1 teaspoon salt
1/4 cup chopped fresh coriander

For vegetable kofta:
1 zucchini grated
2 potatoes, boiled, peeled and mashed
1 teaspoon salt
1/4 cup chopped fresh coriander
1 teaspoon sugar
12x2.5 cubes mature cheese (any kind)
egg and breadcrumbs, for coating
1/2 cup safflower oil, for deep-frying
1 tablespoon cream
chopped fresh coriander, to garnish

To make curry heat oil in pan, saute onion until transparent, add ginger, garlic, saute until golden brown. Add masala paste, fennel, cook for 1 minute, add tomato, crushed almonds, water, stir well. Set aside to cool. Transfer to blender, blend to smooth mixture. Return pan to heat, add blended mixture, bring to boil, simmer for 2 mins, add salt, adjust to taste, bring to boil for 1 minute. Set aside.
To make kofta, squeeze out water from grated zucchini, mix potato, zucchini, salt coriander, sugar. Make 12 balls placing 1 cheese cube inside each ball. Refrigerate for 1 hour. Dip in egg and coat with breadcrumbs, refrigerate for 1 hour. Heat oil in small pan, deep-fry balls few at a time until golden brown, drain on absorbent paper. Keep warm (not hot). Add koftas to heated curry, just before serving. Serve hot, sprinkled with cream and fresh coriander.
To cook ahead: Prepare curry ahead, freeze for 4-6 weeks before using. Prepare koftas 24 hours ahead, refrigerate. Rewarm before adding to heated curry.
Weightwatchers substitute low-fat evaporated milk for cream

Kurlya

KURLYA

(spicy hot curried crabs in coconut milk)

Crab lover's delight, as crabs are cooked in hot and sour creamy coconut sauce.

4 uncooked crabs
2 teaspoons salt
1 teaspoon chilli powder
1 teaspoon turmeric
2 tablespoons safflower oil
3 cloves garlic, finely chopped
1 large onion, finely chopped
coconut sauce (see page 9)
chopped fresh coriander, to garnish

To clean crabs, wash crabs in cold water, twist legs and claws off, set aside, remove and discard hard back and grey feathered gills from crab. Cut crab, in half with kitchen scissors. Use legs and claws as well as body of crab. Mix salt, chilli, turmeric with crabs, toss to coat well. Leave in refrigerator to marinate for 30 mins.
Heat oil in large pan, saute garlic until golden brown. Add onion, saute until light brown. Add crabs, stir on high for 3-4 mins. Reduce heat, cover, cook on low until crabs turn red (approx 2 mins). Add coconut sauce, bring to boil, adjust salt, chilli to taste, remove from heat. Serve hot garnished with fresh coriander, accompanied by boiled rice.
To cook ahead:Prepare 24-48 hours ahead, refrigerate. Reheat on high before serving. Not suitable for freezing.

USAL

(spicy sprouted mung beans)

Coming from a meat & fish eating family and marrying into a vegetarian brahmin family has its advantages. Learning to sprout your own mung beans and to cook them in a delicious combination of garlic & onion is one of them. This recipe taught to me by my mother-in-law is sure to please all palates.

1 cup mung beans (see page 40)
1 tablespoon safflower oil
2 cloves garlic, finely chopped
1 large onion, chopped
2 teaspoons coriander powder
2 teaspoons cumin powder
1 teaspoon turmeric
1 cup water
1 teaspoon salt
1 teaspoon sugar
1 teaspoon chilli powder
1 tablespoon lemon juice
chopped fresh coriander, to garnish

Soak mung beans in 4 cups of hot water overnight, drain, wrap inside tea towel. Preheat oven to 100°C, turn off, place beans inside oven for 24 hours or until mung beans have sprouted (in winter it may take 36 hours).
Heat oil in pan over medium heat, saute garlic until golden brown. Add in onion, saute until transparent. Add sprouted mung beans, coriander and cumin powder, turmeric, stir on high for 1 minute. Add water, bring to boil, cover, simmer on low until mung beans are tender (approx 8 mins), stir occasionally. Add salt, sugar, chilli, lemon juice, cover, cook for 2 mins. Adjust salt, chilli to taste. Serve hot garnished with fresh coriander.
To cook ahead: Prepare ahead, freeze for upto 4-6 weeks before using. Store uncooked sprouted beans in refrigerator for 24-36 hrs in air tight container before use. Uncooked beans not suitable for freezing.

Usal

MEAT KOFTA CURRY

(spicy curry with fried meat balls)

For Curry
1 tablespoon safflower oil
1 large onion, finely chopped
1 teaspoon minced ginger
1 teaspoon minced garlic
1/2 tablespoon Sharwood Tikka masala paste (mixed with 2 teaspoons paprika)
1/2 cup tomato puree ***OR*** *1 small tomato, chopped*
1 cup water
1/2 teaspoon salt
2 tablespoons light cream

For Meat Koftas
200g lean beef, chicken, lamb or pork mince
1 tablespoon chopped fresh coriander
1 egg beaten
1 teaspoon plain flour
1/2 teaspoon chilli powder
1 teaspoon minced ginger
1/2 teaspoon salt
mature cheese (any kind) cut in 12 cubes of 2.5cms each
1/2 cup safflower oil, for deep-drying
chopped fresh coriander, to garnish

To make curry, heat oil in pan, saute onion, until golden brown. Add ginger, garlic, saute until transparent. Add masala paste, stir for 1 minute, remove from heat.
Transfer half of onion to blender, add tomato puree or chopped tomato, water, blend to smooth liquid. Return pan to heat, add blended mixture, salt. Bring to boil, simmer for 2 mins, set aside.
To make koftas, mix all ingredients (except oil and cheese) in bowl. Shape around cheese cube to make small meat balls, approx. 3cm in diameter, refrigerate for 1 hour. Heat oil in pan over medium heat, slip meatballs in oil gently, fry until golden brown. Drain on absorbent paper. Transfer to heated curry. Add cream. Serve hot garnished with fresh coriander, accompanied by boiled rice.
To cook ahead: Prepare ahead and freeze separately for 4-6 weeks. Reheat meatballs separately in oven, add to heated curry and add cream just before serving.
Weightwatchers substitute low-fat evaporated milk for cream.

Meat Kofta Curry, Mattar Pilav, Keshar Pilav

RICE IDEAS

From simple boiled rice to the rich and fragrant Biryani - the maharaja of all rice dishes - rice in India is cooked in a myriad of different ways. Follow these tips to produce moist tender rice dishes every time. Use basmati rice for best results. wash and drain rice before cooking to prevent it becoming sticky. When cooking rice, always use a heavy-based pan to prevent sticking and avoid the temptation to lift the lid while the rice is cooking because precious steam will escape and result in half cooked rice.

Clockwise from top: Moghalai Biryani, Prawn Pilav, Murg Biryani

MOGHALAI BIRYANI

(rice with spicy lamb)

1 kg boneless lamb
2 tablespoons white vinegar
3 teaspoons salt
1/2 cup safflower oil
2 cloves
2 cinnamon sticks
2 whole cardamom
2 large onions, finely chopped
2 teaspoons minced ginger
2 teaspoons minced garlic
2 tablespoons Sharwood medium curry paste
1 teaspoon garam masala (see page 40)
1 small tomato, skinned and chopped
1/4 cup chopped fresh coriander
2 1/2 cup basmati rice, rinsed and drained
5 cups boiling water
To garnish
100 grams cashew nuts, to serve
1/4 cup sultana, to serve
1x100g packet fried onion, (see page 40)

Trim excess fat from lamb, cut into 5 cm pieces, marinate in mixture of vinegar, 2 tsp salt. Leave in refrigerator for 2 hours.
Heat oil in pan, add cloves, cinnamon, cardamom, when cloves pop, add onion, saute until transparent. Add ginger, garlic, saute until golden brown. Add curry paste, garam masala, cook for 1 minute, stir constantly. Add tomato, stir until thick paste is formed. Add lamb pieces, mix well, cook on high for 2 mins, cover, cook on low until lamb is tender (approx 35-40 mins). Add coriander, stir until excess water evaporates. Adjust salt to taste. Remove meat from pan, set aside. Leave about 2 tablespoon paste in pan, add rice, stir for 30 seconds. Add water, 1 tsp salt, bring to boil, cover, simmer on low until rice is cooked (approx 20 mins). All water should be absorbed by now.
To prepare garnish, heat 1 tablespoon safflower oil in pan, saute cashew nuts until golden brown. Set aside. Repeat with sultanas. Spread half of cooked rice evenly over base of serving dish, top with prepared lamb, place rest of rice evenly on top. Garnish with cashew nuts, sultana and onions.
To cook ahead: Prepare ahead, refrigerate. Reheat in covered casserole dish at 150°C for 45 mins to 1 hour or in microwave.

PRAWN PILAV

(spicy rice with prawns)

500g uncooked, shelled prawns
2 teaspoons salt
1 teaspoon turmeric
1 teaspoon tamarind concentrate
2 tablespoons safflower oil
1 large onion, finely chopped
2 teaspoons minced ginger
2 teaspoons minced garlic
2 cups basmati rice, rinsed and drained
1 teaspoon chilli powder
2 teaspoons cinnamon powder
4 cups boiling water
1/2 cup instant coconut milk powder
chopped fresh coriander, to garnish

Devein prawns and wash. Mix salt, turmeric, tamarind in bowl, add prawns, toss to coat, leave to marinate in refrigerator for 4-6 hours. Heat oil in pan, saute onion, until transparent. Add garlic, ginger, saute until golden brown. Add prawns, rice, chilli, cinnamon, stir for 30 seconds. Add boiling water, coconut powder, adjust salt, chilli to taste, bring to boil, cover, simmer on low until all water is absorbed (30 mins approx) and rice is cooked. Serve hot with fresh coriander.
To cook ahead: Freezes for up to 4-6 weeks. Thaw in refrigerator and heat in oven at 150°C for 45 mins. Suitable for microwave heating.

MURG BIRYANI

(rice with spicy chicken)

1 kg chicken thighs, skinless
1 cup yogurt
3 teaspoons salt
3 tablespoons Sharwood medium curry paste
1/2 cup safflower oil
2 cloves
2 cinnamon sticks
2 whole cardamom
2 large onions, finely chopped
3 teaspoons garam masala (see page 40)
3 medium tomatoes, chopped
1/4 cup chopped fresh coriander
2 1/2 cups basmati rice, rinsed and drained
5 cups boiling water
1x100gms fried onions (see page 40)
2 hard boiled eggs

Trim excess fat from chicken, cut each thigh in 3 small pieces. Mix chicken, yogurt, 1 1/2 teaspoons salt, only 1 tablespoon curry paste in bowl, toss to coat, marinate in refrigerator for 12 hours. Place chicken pieces on foil-lined tray, brown on both sides under hot grill. This helps to seal juices.
Heat oil in large thick based pan, add cloves, cinnamon, cardamom. As cloves pop, add onion, saute until golden brown, add remaining curry paste, garam masala, stir for 1 minute. Add tomato, stir until thick paste is formed. Add browned chicken, juices from tray, stir for 2 mins on high, cover, cook on low until chicken is cooked through (approx 8 mins). Add coriander, stir on high to remove excess liquid. Remove chicken from pan, set aside. Leave approximately 2 tablespoons of paste in pan, return pan to heat, add rice, stir for 30 seconds, add boiling water and remaining salt, mix well, bring to boil, adjust salt to taste, cover, simmer on low until all water is absorbed (approximately 20 mins) and rice is cooked. Spread half of rice evenly on base of serving dish, top evenly with prepared chicken, spread remaining rice evenly on top. Garnish with sliced boiled egg and sprinkle with fried onion.
To cook ahead: Prepare ahead,freeze for 4-6 weeks without garnish, thaw in refrigerator, reheat in oven at 150°C for 45 mins. Garnish just before serving. Serve with papadam and raita of your choice (see page 29).

SABZI PILAV

(rice with mixed vegetables)

This vegetable pilav is a must in wedding feasts in Bombay and its surrounding districts. Served with numerous traditional wedding sweets, it's hot and spicy taste makes a welcome contrast (relief).

2 cups basmati rice, rinsed and drained
1 large eggplant cut in 2.5 cm pieces
12 cauliflower floret
1 large potato, peeled, cut into 2.5cm cubes
1/4 cup safflower oil
2 teaspoons garam masala (see page 40)
2 teaspoons cumin powder
2 teaspoons coriander powder
1/2 teaspoon chilli powder
1 tablespoon dessicated coconut
1 teaspoon turmeric
1/2 teaspoon chopped fresh coriander
2 tablespoons natural yogurt
4 cups boiling water
chopped fresh coriander, to garnish

Heat oil in pan, over medium heat. Add all ingredients, except water, stir for 1 minute. Add boiling water, add salt to taste, bring to boil, cover, simmer on low until all the water is absorbed (approx 20-25 mins) and rice is cooked. Serve hot garnished with fresh coriander.
To cook ahead: Prepare 24-48 hours ahead and refrigerate. Reheat at 150°C for 45 mins. Not suitable for freezing.

CHOLE PILAV

(rice with chickpeas)

1/4 cup chickpeas ***OR*** *1/2 cup canned cooked chickpeas*
1 cup basmati rice, rinsed and drained
1 tablespoon safflower oil
1 stick cinnamon
1 clove
2 cups of water

If using uncooked chickpeas, see page 13 to cook them. Heat oil in pan over medium heat, add cinnamon,clove. As clove pops, reduce heat add rice, stir for 30 seconds. Add chickpeas, water, bring to boil, cover, simmer on low until all water has been absorbed and rice is cooked (approx 15 mins). Remove cinnamon, clove, serve hot.
To cook ahead: Prepare ahead, freeze for 4-6 weeks. Thaw in refrigerator. Reheat in covered casserole dish at 120°C for 30 mins.
Variation of the above recipe (instead of chick peas) use:-

Gajjar Pilav
1 small carrot, peeled and chopped

Mattar Pilav
1/2 cup frozen peas

Chole Pilav, Sabzi Pilav

KHICHADI

(rice with sprouted beans)

1 cup brown lentil
2 cups basmati rice, rinsed and drained
1 teaspoon ginger
1 teaspoon garlic
2 tablespoons safflower oil
1 inch cinnamon stick
2 cloves
2 whole pepper corn
3 bay leaves
1 teaspoon turmeric
1 large onion, finely chopped
1 tablespoon garam masala (see page 40)
1 teaspoon sugar
1 teaspoon salt
1 teaspoon chilli powder or 1 fresh green chilli, chopped
6 cups water

Sprout lentils as in mung usal (see page 20). Wash sprouted lentils, drain and mix with rice and ginger, garlic in bowl. Set aside for 2 hours. Heat oil in a heavy based pan, add cinnamon, clove, pepper corn, bay leaves. As they pop add onion, saute until transparent, add rice and lentils and rest of the ingredients, except water, stir for 2 mins, add water, bring to boil, adjust salt to taste. Cover, simmer on low until all water has been absorbed and rice is cooked (approx 35 mins). Remove cinnamon, bay leaves before serving. Serve hot with your choice of raita (see page 29).
To cook ahead: Suitable to freeze for 4-6 weeks. Thaw in refrigerator and reheat in covered casserole at 150°C for 45 mins. Suitable for microwave heating.

SAFED CHAWAL

(boiled rice)

1 tablespoon safflower oil
1 cup basmati rice, rinsed and drained
2 cups water

Heat oil in pan over medium heat, add rice to pan, stir for 30 seconds. Add water, bring to boil, cover, simmer on low for 15-20 mins or until all water is absorbed and rice is cooked. Serve hot.
To cook ahead: Suitable to freeze for 4-6 weeks. Thaw in refrigerator. Reheat in covered casserole dish at 120°C for 30 mins.

KESHAR PILAV

(saffron rice)

1 tablespoon safflower oil
1/4 teaspoon cumin seeds (optional)
1 1/2 cup basmati rice, rinsed and drained
3 cups water
3 strands saffron (optional)
pinch of yellow colour (see page 40)

Heat oil in pan, add cumin seeds (if using), stir until they turn black, add rice, stir for 30 seconds. Add water, saffron (if using), yellow colour, bring to boil, cover, simmer on low until rice is cooked (approx 15-20 mins). All water should be absorbed by now. Serve hot.
To cook ahead:Suitable to freeze for 4-6 weeks. Thaw in refrigerator. Reheat in covered casserole dish at 120°C for 30 mins.

BREAD

The diversity of breads which make up the staple of every Indian meal is mind boggling. Here, I have included three Indian bread recipes, which are both nutritious and easy to prepare. Ready made Lapinja and Phoenician breads make fine substitutes and are easily available from super markets and delicatessens. Recipes serve four.

Clockwise from left: Phoenician Bread, Lapinja Bread, Bhatoore, Paratha, Gobi&Palak Paratha

BHATOORE

(fried Indian bread)

2 cups self-raising flour
1 tablespoon safflower oil
1/2 cup natural yogurt
1/2 teaspoon salt
1/4 teaspoon sugar
1/2 cup water
1 cup safflower oil, for deep-frying

Place flour in bowl, make well in centre, add oil, yogurt, salt, sugar, mix well. Slowly add enough water to make pizza-like dough, rub little oil on your hands, knead dough until smooth. Set aside in air tight container at room temperature for 6 hours.
With a little oil on your hands knead dough to make it very smooth. divide into 20 balls. On lightly-oiled baking paper roll out each ball into thin bhatoora 5 cms in diameter, using rolling pin. Heat oil in fry-pan over medium heat, slip bhatoora into oil, deep-fry on both sides until golden brown, drain on absorbent paper, serve hot.
To cook ahead: Prepare dough 24 to 48 hours ahead and refrigerate in airtight container. Roll bhatoore couple of hours ahead. For best results, fry just before serving.

LAPINJA BREAD

2 lapinja bread

Cut each bread into 5 slices, wrap in foil, warm in oven at 150°C for 20 minutes before serving.
To cook ahead: Cut bread and wrap in foil and freeze ready for use. Thaw before warming.

PARATHA

(flat wholemeal bread)

2 cups wholemeal flour (atta)
1 cup water
1/4 cup safflower oil
2 tablespoons plain flour
1 tablespoon unsalted butter

Place flour in bowl, slowly add enough water to make firm dough (you might need more flour or water), sprinkle 2 teaspoon oil on dough, knead until dough is very smooth (use food processor for this step if preferred). Set aside in airtight container for 4-6 hours.
To make paratha, sprinkle 2 teaspoon oil on dough, knead once again until dough is soft and smooth (unlike pastry, Indian bread dough gives better results if kneaded really well). Shape into 14 golf size balls. On kitchen paper place plain flour to use while rolling parathas. Coat dough ball with flour, roll out a square approx 10x10cms, brush top with oil, fold to make a rectangular parcel, as in picture. Brush with oil each time before folding. Coat parcel with flour, roll out into a square 14x14 cm to make paratha. Repeat with remaining dough balls and spread them out on kitchen paper.
Heat nonstick fry pan over low to medium heat, brush lightly with oil, cook paratha until small bubbles appear on surface (approx 40-50 seconds), turn with spatula, cook under side until golden brown (approx 50 seconds) before turning once more and pressing gently all over with spatula until golden brown. Paratha should puff as it cooks. Remove from pan, brush with butter, stack on top of each other. Serve hot.
To cook ahead: Prepare parathas ahead and freeze in freezer bag, wrapped in foil. Will keep for 6 weeks. Thaw and reheat in oven at 120° C for 45 minutes. Not suitable for refrigeration.

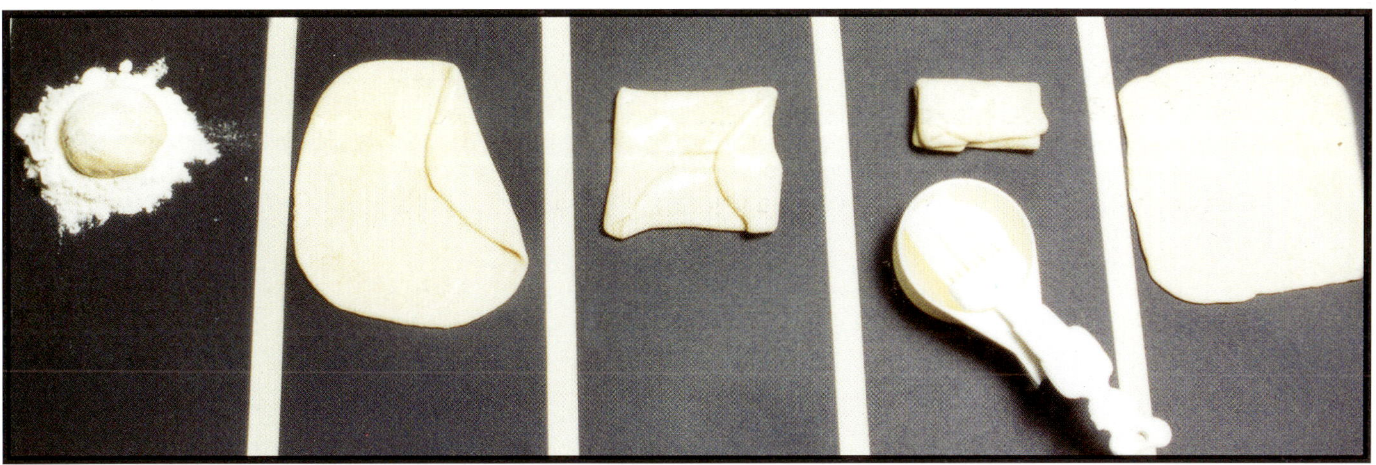

Making of Paratha

GOBI PALAK PARATHA

(flat stuffed cabbage spinach bread)

1 teaspoon safflower oil
1 1/2 cup grated cabbage
1/4 cup cooked spinach
1/4 cup chopped fresh coriander
1 teaspoon salt
1/4 teaspoon turmeric
1/4 teaspoon chilli powder (optional)
1/4 teaspoon sugar
3/4 cup wholemeal flour
unsalted butter

Heat oil in nonstick pan, add all ingredients (except flour), stir, cover, cook on low until cabbage is well cooked (approx 5-7mins), stir occasionally. increase heat to cook off excess water. Keep aside to cool.
Add flour slowly to cooled vegetable mixture, kneading all the time to make firm dough. Wet hand with little oil, and knead the dough to smooth texture. Keep aside in airtight container at room temperature for 4-6 hours.
To make paratha, knead dough well, divide into 10 balls. Dip ball in plain flour, on greased paper roll round paratha 5 cms diameter using rolling pin. Sprinkle with a little plain flour while rolling to prevent sticking. Cook as in above recipe. Brush with butter, stack on top of each other. Serve hot.
To cook ahead: Prepare parathas ahead and freeze in freezer bag, wrapped in foil, for upto 4-6 weeks. Thaw and reheat in oven at 120°C for 45 minutes. Not suitable for refrigeration.

PHOENICIAN BREAD

4 phoenician bread
1 tablespoon unsalted butter or margarine

Cut each bread in 4 pieces, butter one side, wrap in foil, heat in oven at 150°C for 30 minutes. Serve hot.

RAITAS

Natural yogurt, known as Dahi or curd is indispensable to the preparation of an Indian meal. When yogurt is mixed with finely sliced or grated raw or cooked vegetables, it is known as Raita. A natural antacid against chilli, raita is a cooling and palate-cleansing counterpoint to the rich and spicy dishes it accompanies. Recipes serve four.

Clockwise from top: Kuchumber, Salad hindustani & Pachadi

PACHADI

(sliced tomato and banana in yogurt)

1/2 teaspoon safflower oil
1/4 teaspoon cumin seeds
1/2 cup natural yogurt
2 large tomatoes, finely chopped
1 large banana
1/4 teaspoon salt
chopped fresh coriander, to garnish

Heat oil in pan, add cumin seeds, as they turn dark, remove pan, set aside to cool. Mix yogurt with tomato and cumin in a serving bowl, refrigerate. Just before serving, add sliced banana and salt. Serve cold, garnished with fresh coriander.

SALAD HINDUSTANI

(fresh vegetables sprinkled with herbs and spices)

1 large tomato
1 spanish onion
3 radishes
2 lebanese cucumbers
1 tablespoon lemon juice
1/4 teaspoon salt
1/4 teaspoon cumin powder

Thinly slice tomato, onion, radishes and cucumber. Arrange vegetables on serving platter and refrigerate. Mix lemon juice with salt and cumin, refrigerate. Sprinkle dressing on salad just before serving. Serve cold.
To cook ahead: Prepare 6-8 hours ahead and refrigerate covered with gladwrap.

KUCHUMBAR

(spicy mixed vegetable salad)

1 large tomato. finely chopped
1 spanish onion, finely chopped
1/2 cucumber, finely chopped
1 small green chilli, finely chopped (optional)
1/4 cup chopped fresh coriander
1/4 teaspoon salt

Mix all ingredients (except salt) in serving bowl and refrigerate. Stir in salt just before serving, serve cold.
To cook ahead: Prepare 6-8 hours ahead and refrigerate. Not suitable for freezing.

KADOO RAITA

(pumpkin in yogurt)

1/2 teaspoon safflower oil
1/4 teaspoon cumin seeds
250g pumpkin, peeled, cooked and mashed
1/2 cup natural yogurt
dash hot mustard
1/4 cup chopped fresh coriander
1/4 teaspoon salt

Heat oil in small pan, add cumin seeds, as they turn dark remove pan, set aside to cool. Mix pumpkin with yogurt, mustard, coriander in serving bowl and refrigerate. Add salt just before serving, sprinkle with cumin seeds. Serve cold.
To cook ahead: Prepare 6-8 hours ahead and refrigerate. Not suitable for freezing.

RAITA KHIRA

(grated cucumber in yogurt)

1/2 continental cucumber, grated
1/2 cup natural yogurt
1 tablespoon chopped fresh coriander
1/2 teaspoon safflower oil
1/4 teaspoon cumin seeds
1/4 teaspoon salt

Mix cucumber with yogurt, coriander in serving bowl, refrigerate. Heat oil in pan, add cumin seeds, as they turn black, set aside to cool, add to mixture. Add salt just before serving. Serve cold.
To cook ahead: Prepare 4-6 hours ahead.

ALOO RAITA

(potato in yogurt)

1 teaspoon safflower oil
1/4 teaspoon brown mustard seeds (see page 40)
1/4 teaspoon turmeric
2 medium potatoes, boiled, peeled, cut in 1 cm pieces
1/2 cup natural yogurt
1/4 teaspoon salt
pinch sugar
1 tablespoon crushed peanuts
chopped fresh coriander, to garnish

Heat oil in pan, add mustard seeds, as they pop add turmeric, set aside to cool. Mix potato, yogurt and mustard seeds in serving bowl, refrigerate. Add salt, sugar, peanuts just before serving. Serve cold garnished with fresh coriander.

KHAMANG KAKADI

(grated cucumber with crushed peanut)

1 teaspoon safflower oil
1/4 teaspoon cumin seeds
1 cucumber, grated
1/4 teaspoon salt
1/4 teaspoon sugar
1/2 teaspoon lemon juice
1 tablespoon crushed peanuts
chopped fresh coriander, to garnish

Heat oil in pan, add cumin seeds, as they turn black, remove pan, set aside to cool. Mix cucumber with cumin in a bowl and refrigerate. Just before serving, add salt, sugar, lemon juice, crushed peanuts, mix well. Serve cold garnished with fresh coriander.

Clockwise from top left: Aloo Raita, Khamang Kakadi, Raita Khira, Kadoo Raita

CHUTNEYS AND PICKLES

A selection of chutneys and pickles to suit every palate - sour, hot, or sweet - is an essential accompaniment to every Indian meal. As well as complementing the main course, they stimulate appetite and aid digestion. Colourful pickles and chutneys look striking displayed in tall glass jars and make wonderful gifts for family and friends.

From left to right, Top: Chilli Pickle, Date chutney
Middle: Coconut Coriander chutney, Mixed Vegetable Pickle, Lemon Pickle 1
Bottom: Lemon Pickle 2, Mint Chutney, Coconut Garlic Chutney

MIXED VEGETABLE PICKLE

2 tablespoons salt
2 cups warm water
1/2 cup cauliflower, finely chopped
1/2 cup carrots, finely chopped
1/2 cup green beans, finely chopped
1/4 cup safflower oil
1/4 cup brown mustard seeds (see page 40)
1 teaspoon fenugreek seeds (see page 40)
1/4 cup lemon juice
2 teaspoons chilli powder
1/2 teaspoon sugar
1 teaspoon turmeric
1/4 cup vinegar

Mix 2 teaspoons salt with warm water in bowl, soak vegetables overnight, drain. Spread vegetables out on clean tea towel to dry. Heat oil in pan, add 1 teaspoon mustard seeds. As they pop, set aside to cool in their oil. Place remaining mustard seeds and fenugreek seeds in dry grinder and grind to very fine powder. Transfer to bowl with lemon juice, chilli, remaining salt, sugar and turmeric and beat until fluffy. Add drained vegetables and mix well to combine. Stir in vinegar and cooled mustard seeds with their oil into vegetable mixture. Transfer pickle to clean dry glass jar, refrigerate for 3-4 days, stirring couple of times. Adjust salt to taste and serve.
Hint: Store in a glass jar in the refrigerator for 4-6 months. For really hot pickle add extra teaspoon of chilli powder. Not suitable for freezing.

DATE CHUTNEY

1/2 cup pitted dates
1 cup boiling water
1 tablespoon tamarind concentrate (see page 40)
1/4 teaspoon salt
1/4 teaspoon chilli powder
1/4 teaspoon cumin powder

Soak dates in boiling water for 2-4 hours. Transfer to food processor or blender, puree and strain. Mix date puree with remaining ingredients in serving bowl, refrigerate until ready to use.
Hint: Can keep in the refrigerator for up to 7 days.

COCONUT CORIANDER CHUTNEY

1/2 cup chopped fresh coriander
1 green chilli, chopped
1/2 cup dessicated coconut
3 tablespoons natural yogurt
1/2 teaspoon salt
1/2 teaspoon sugar

Freeze coriander and chilli solid. Transfer to a dry grinder, add coconut and process to very fine powder. Transfer to serving bowl, mix with yogurt, salt, sugar. Adjust salt to taste, refrigerate until ready to serve.
Hint: Use chilli powder if green chilli is not available (although the result will not be as green) Prepare 4-6 weeks ahead and freeze until ready to use. Add a little water to soften if thawed mixture is too thick.

COCONUT AND GARLIC CHUTNEY

1 garlic leaf, chopped (see page 40)
1 small green chilli chopped
1/2 cup dessicated coconut
3 tablespoons natural yogurt
1/2 teaspoon salt
pinch sugar

Freeze garlic and chilli solid. Transfer to dry grinder, add coconut and process to a fine powder. Transfer to serving bowl,, mix with yogurt, salt, sugar. Refrigerate until ready to serve.
Hint: If garlic leaf is not available, substitute 1 small clove of garlic (chopped and frozen). Prepare ahead and freeze until ready to serve. Add1 or 2 tablespoon yogurt or water if thawed mixture is too thick.

CHILLI PICKLE

1/2 cup safflower oil
1/2 cup brown mustard seeds
2 teaspoons turmeric
250g green chillies, washed
3 teaspoons fenugreek seeds
1/2 cup lemon juice
1/2 cup salt

Heat oil in small pan, add only 2 teaspoons mustard seeds. As they pop, add turmeric, remove from heat, set aside to cool. Using kitchen towel, dry chillies thoroughly, remove stalks, chop finely. In dry grinder, grind fenugreek seeds and remaining mustard seeds to a very fine powder. Transfer to a bowl, add lemon juice and beat until fluffy. Add chillies, salt, mix well. Add cooled oil to chilli mixture, mix, transfer to clean, dry, wide-necked jar, cover and refrigerate for 2 weeks. Adjust salt, lemon juice to taste.
Hint: Keep in the refrigerator for upto 1 year. Wear rubber gloves while chopping chillies to avoid irritating your skin.

LEMON PICKLE 1

4 lemons, washed, dried, skin left on and coarsely chopped
2 teaspoons salt
2 teaspoons chilli powder
4 tablespoons sugar
1/4 cup dried black currant

Mix lemon, salt, chilli, sugar, black currants in bowl. Transfer, to a wide-necked, clean, dry, glass jar. Cover and leave in the sun to marinate for 1 month (perhaps longer if there are not too many sunny days), stir every two days. Keeps in the refrigerator for 1 year..

MINT CHUTNEY

1 cup chopped fresh mint leaves
1/2 cup chopped fresh coriander
1/4 cup lemon juice
1/2 teaspoon salt
1/2 or 1 green chilli

Blend all ingredients in a food processor or blender to a fine paste. Refrigerate until ready to serve. Add 1 tablespoon natural yogurt for a creamier variation.
To cook ahead: Prepare 24-48 hours ahead and refrigerate. Not suitable for freezing.

PAPADAMS

These are made from lentils, the main ingredients being Udad daal, and are available in shops in flavours ranging from mild to very hot.
Papadams are served as savoury snacks with drinks as well as a crispy accompaniment, to the main meal.
To cook, heat 1/4 cup oil in fry pan over medium heat. Slip papadams into oil one at a time and deep-fry until done.
For microwave cooking approximately 10 seconds (on high) per papadam

LEMON PICKLE 2

4 lemons
2 teaspoons salt
1/2 teaspoon fenugreek seeds (see page 40)
2 teaspoons chilli powder
1/2 teaspoon turmeric
6 tablespoons sugar
1/2 cup boiling water

Wash and coarsely chop lemons, leaving skin on, remove the pips. Place lemons, salt in bowl, mix well. Set aside for 1 hour. Heat a non-stick pan, dry roast fenugreek seeds until golden brown. Transfer to dry grinder, add chilli, turmeric, sugar and grind to very fine powder. Heat pan over low heat, add lemons with their juice, cook covered for 10 mins or until skins are tender. Remove lemons from pan, set aside. Return pan to heat, add water, prepared powder, cook for 2 mins. Return lemons to pan, cook on low, stirring for 5-7 mins or until thickened. Remove from heat, adjust salt, chilli to taste. Cool and transfer to a clean, dry glass jar.It is ready for use. Keeps in the refrigerator for up to 1 year.

DESSERTS

Most of the Indian desserts are a treat for sweet-tooths. This choice of three desserts are simple to prepare and chosen especially to suit the less sweet preferences of the western palate. The recipes are for four.

Clockwise from left: Gajjar Halwa, Gulab Jamun & Trikhand

GULAB JAMUN

(fried balls in sugar syrup)

For milk balls
3/4 cup full cream milk powder
1/4 cup self-raising flour
1/4 cup light thickened cream
1 cup safflower oil, for deep-frying

For syrup
2 cups water
1 cup sugar
2 strands of saffron
pinch of yellow colour (see page 40)

To make milk balls, mix milk powder, flour in bowl until well combined, add cream slowly to make smooth soft dough. Knead for 2-3 minutes or until dough is of very smooth texture (if dough is crumbly you may need little more cream). Shape into 12 smooth balls, set aside. Heat oil in small nonstick pan over low heat (it will be hot enough when little dough added to pan bubbles up to surface). Slip milk balls into oil 3 or 4 at a time, deep-fry stirring gently with wooden spatula, until swollen to twice their size (approx 2 minutes). Prick each ball gently with fork, continue deep-frying until golden brown. Drain on absorbent paper.
To make syrup, mix water, sugar in pan over medium heat until sugar is completely dissolved. Stir in saffron and colour, remove from heat. Add milk balls, stir gently to coat with syrup, set aside for 2-3 hours to soak up syrup. Serve warm or cold.

HINT: All the desserts can be prepared 2-3 days ahead and refrigerated. They are unsuitable for freezing.

Weightwatchers Unfortunately these recipes are not suitable for substitution with low-fat ingredients. So watch out!!! Perhaps just a spoonful ???

GAJJAR HALWA

(grated carrot in sweetened cream and butter)

1 tablespoon unsalted butter
4 cups grated carrot
1 1/2 cups thickened cream
1/2 cup sugar
10 strands saffron
1/4 teaspoon freshly powdered cardamom
Almond silvers, for garnish

Melt butter in nonstick pan over medium heat, add carrot, cream, cook for 5 minutes. Add sugar, saffron and cardamom, stir for 12-15 minutes, until cream reduces. Halwa is ready when butter begins separating and mixture is dry. Transfer to serving bowl, garnish with almond silvers and serve warm or cold.

TRIKHAND

(sweet saffron yogurt with fruits)

1/4 cup sugar
4-6 strands saffron
1/4 teaspoon cardamom seeds
60x60cm square muslin cloth
2 cups European Style natural yogurt
1 cup mango slices, drained
1 punnet strawberries
1 small red, delicious apple
1 kiwi fruit, peeled and thinly sliced, for garnish

To make saffron sugar, grind sugar, saffron, cardamom pods to very fine powder in dry grinder, keep aside.
To make chakka, drape muslin over sieve, spoon yogurt in centre of cloth, draw four corners together, secure with string, set aside to drain overnight (over kitchen sink is ideal). Thick yogurt which remains following morning is called chakka. Using hand-held or electric beater, mix chakka with saffron sugar until sugar dissolves and mixture yellows evenly. Refrigerate. Cut mango, strawberries, apple in small pieces, gently mix with yogurt. Garnish with kiwi fruit and serve cold. Alternatively make fruit salad (using mango, apple, kiwi and strawberry) and serve with blob of saffron yogurt garnished with strawberry.

FINGER FOODS

Spicy and moreish, this selection of savoury Indian treats, travel well and are simple to reheat and serve. Savoury hot and spicy snacks are served in every Indian household. I have adapted some of these to suit our Aussie kitchens. For more finger food ideas, see recipes for Karanjee, Batatawada, Sabzi Kabab, Samosa and Machi Kabab.

Clockwise from top: Indian Pizza, Indian Omlette Tart. Tandoori Sandwiches, Namkin Machi, Namkin Gobi

INDIAN OMELETTE TARTS

(pastry tarts with spicy omelette filling

1/2x750g packet Vidal's shortcrust pastry mix
For filling
1 tablespoon safflower oil
1 small onion, finely chopped
1/2 teaspoon minced ginger
3 eggs beaten
1/2 cup grated mature cheese (any kind)
1/4 teaspoon salt
freshly ground black pepper
1/2 cup chopped fresh coriander

Make pastry according to packet instructions. Divide dough into 10 balls. On lightly floured surface, roll out pastry to 5 mm thick , cut out rounds using 6-7 cm pastry cutter (approx 40 rounds). Place rounds in lightly oiled patty tins, set aside. To make filling, heat oil in pan, saute onion, ginger until transparent. Set aside to cool. Mix onions, ginger with eggs, cheese, salt, pepper, coriander, adjust salt, pepper to taste, spoon into prepared pastry cases. Bake for 10-12 minutes at 200°C or until golden brown. Serve warm or cold.
To cook ahead: Freeze for 4-6 weeks before use. Reheat, uncovered, for 30 minutes at 120°C.

NAMKIN MACHI

(spicy tuna slice)

1x425g tin tuna in brine, drained
2 cups chopped spinach, cooked or 200g frozen spinach, thawed
1/250g box water cracker biscuits (any kind), crushed
1 onion, finely chopped
1 teaspoon minced ginger
1 teaspoon minced garlic
1/2 teaspoon chilli powder
1/2 cup chopped fresh coriander
3 eggs, beaten
1/4 teaspoon salt
1 cup grated mature cheese, any kind

Mix all ingredients in bowl, adjust salt to taste, press into lightly oiled 24x24cm baking tin, bake for 45-50 minutes at 250°C or until tops are golden brown. Set aside to cool, cut into squares, serve warm or cold.
To cook ahead: Prepare 24-48 hours ahead and refrigerate. Not suitable for freezing.
Vegetarian Variation:
Namkin Gobi (spicy cabbage slice)
Substitute 4 cups of finely chopped cabbage for tuna and proceed as above.

INDIAN PIZZAS

For Pizza Base
1 kg packet white bread mix

For topping
2 tablespoons safflower oil
2 large onions, finely chopped
2 large tomatoes, finely chopped
1/2 cup cooked spinach
2 tablespoons Sharwood hot curry paste
1 teaspoon salt
300g lean beef, chicken, lamb or pork mince (optional)
1/2 cup chopped fresh coriander
400g mushrooms, finely chopped (optional)
2 large green capsicums, seeded and finely chopped
1 large red capsicum, seeded and finely chopped
grated mozzarella cheese. to serve

Prepare bread dough according to packet instructions, sprinkle 1 tablespoon oil, turn onto lightly floured surface, knead until dough is of very smooth texture. Transfer dough to very large airtight container, set aside in warm place for 1 hour. Dough will rise to double its size. Moisten hands with little oil, divide dough into 50 equal balls and roll out each ball into thin pizza base 7-8 cm in diameter, with rolling pin.
To make topping, heat 2 teaspoon oil in pan, saute onion until transparent. Add tomato, spinach, curry paste, salt, mince (if using), stir for 2 minutes. Continue to cook until all water evaporates. Add coriander, adjust salt to taste, set aside to cool. Place pizzas on lightly oiled oven trays, cover evenly with topping, sprinkle with chopped capsicum, mushroom (if using), top with cheese, bake for 10-12 minutes at 250°C. or until crisp and golden brown.
To cook ahead: Freeze for up to 4-6 weeks before using. Reheat for 15-20 minutes at 150°C.

TANDOORI SANDWICHES

500g boneless chicken, skinned
1 cup natural yogurt
1 teaspoon salt
2 tablespoons Sharwood tandoori paste
bread, for sandwiches
coconut garlic chutney, to serve (see page 33)

Trim excess fat from chicken, pierce all over with fork. Mix chicken with yogurt, salt, tandoori paste, marinate in refrigerator for 12-18 hours. Place chicken on foil-lined tray, brown chicken on both sides under hot grill. Transfer to oven, bake covered for 30 minutes at 200 °C, set aside to cool. Chop chicken thinly. Makes 16-20 sandwiches. Spread one side with coconut garlic chutney for extra spice.
To cook ahead: Freeze sandwiches for 4-6 weeks. Thaw in refrigerator. Alternatively, freeze cooked chicken for 4-6 weeks, thaw in refrigerator and use to make sandwiches as required.

MENUS

Planning a menu for a family meal or for entertaining can be very tedious as one has to consider interesting dishes combining the time factor. Being a professional, I have found that planning a menu is a very essential part of cooking. This planning has allowed me to present interesting and well balanced meals to my family and friends with a minimum of fuss. A happy meal time is one of the most important parts of a happy family life. The following menus are for 4.

Clockwise from top: Pilav (Mattar, Keshar, Gajjar), Kadoo Raita, Zinga Kadhi, Meat Kofta Curry

VEGETARIAN MENUS

Sabzi Kabab (Vegetable patties)
Rajma (Red kidney beans in spicy sauce)
Gobi Maka (cabbage with corn)
Gajjar Pilav (rice with carrots)
Paratha (flat wholemeal bread)
Salad Hindustani (fresh vegetables sprinkled with herbs and spices)
Pickle of your choice
Papadam
Gulab Jamun (fried milk balls in sugar syrup)

Batata Wada (potato balls in spicy lentil batter)
Sabzi Damayanti (mixed vegetables in cream sauce)
Daal Maheshwari (spicy mixed lentils)
Chole Pilav (rice with chickpeas)
Bhatoore (fried indian bread)
Pachadi (sliced tomato and banana in yogurt)
Pickle of your choice
Papadam
Gajjar Halwa (grated carrot in sweetened cream and butter)

NONVEGETARIAN MENUS

Machi Kabab (fish patties)
Murg Dahiwala (chicken in yogurt)
Chole (chickpeas in garlic sauce)
Mattar Pilav (rice with peas)
Paratha (flat wholemeal bread)
Salad Hindustani (fresh vegetables sprinkled with herbs and spices)
Pickle of your choice
Papadam
Gulab Jamun (fried milk balls in sugar syrup)

Murg Tikka (chicken on skewers)
Gosh Kashmiri (spicy curried lamb with tomato)
Daal Methi (curried lentils with fenugreek & spinach)
Keshar Pilav (saffron rice)
Phoenician Bread
Raita Khira (grated cucumber in yogurt)
Pickle of your choice
Papadam
Trikhand (sweet saffron yogurt with fruits)

Vegetarian Quick Menus

Khichadi **OR** Sabzi Pilav
Raita of your choice
Papadam

Nonvegetarian Quick Menus

Murg Biryani **OR** Moghalai Biryani **OR** Prawn Pilav
Raita of your choice
Papadam

GLOSSARY

Black Eyed Beans: also called lobia, available in most super markets, are a valuable source of protein and have a high fibre content.

Mustard Seeds (whole): are available as brown or white. Brown seeds are preferred as they have stronger anti-flatulent property. Mustard seeds pop when added to hot oil releasing flavour and the beneficial effect of mustard.

Chick Peas: Also called chana, chola or Bengal gram, available in super markets either as dried legume or in cans (cooked). As they take a long time to cook, soak them overnight before boiling. Chick pea has easily digestible protein and high calcium and phosphorus content which is good for bones.

Cumin seeds: White or greenish brown seeds resembling caraway seeds, are used as whole or ground, giving a distinct aroma. Seeds and ground cumin are readily available in supermarkets. When using seeds, always wait till they turn dark after adding to hot oil, to release the flavour and the beneficial effect of cumin.

Dried fenugreek leaves: Available in packets, are used as a herb.

Fennel: also called saunf. Brownish green seeds resembling large caraway seeds, used as whole in pickles or ground giving pleasant and soothing taste. Used as mouth freshener after a spicy Indian meal.

Fenugreek Seeds: Tawny colour seeds, have bitter taste, are used sparingly to give special flavour to daals, vegetables and pickles. Fenugreek plant is easy to grow in your backyard by planting fenugreek seeds. Fresh leaves of the plant are also used in daal and vegetables.

Fried onion crisps: available in shops that specialise in Asian spices and some supermarkets.

Garam Masala: Literally means fresh or hot mixture of ground spices and is a mixture of ground cinnamon, cloves, cardamom, peppercorn, cumin, and/or coriander, available in super markets.

Garlic Leaf: clove or garlic when planted , gives out a green stalk (similar to spring onion). Has a very subtle garlic flavour, gives a fresh green colour to the chutney. Garlic stalk is easy to grow in your backyard by planting a clove of garlic, when planted at the base of roses, it keeps the aphids away. Remove young green stalks, wash, chop and place in deep freezer in plastic bag ready to use.

Masura or Brown Lentils: unskinned legume, available in super markets. Sprouted masura have extra nutritious value.

Mung Beans: green in colour, due to their skin, mung beans are rich in vitamins A, B and C, and niacin. They are also very heat stable. Sprouted mung beans have more nutritional value.

Mung Daal: skinned and split mung beans. It is yellow in colour and is smaller than split pea and oval in shape.

Red Lentils: skinned and split brown lentils, are red in colour and are round in shape. They are available in most super markets

Saffron: Rather expensive spice, has special flavour and colour. Saffron is sold as orange coloured strands and used in sweets and rice preparations.

Split Pea: this is ordinary yellow split pea, available in most super markets and used commonly to make lentil soup.

Splitpea flour: Flour made from yellow split pea, is pale yellow. Besan or chickpea flours can be substituted for splitpea flour. Split pea flour is used to make batter, to thicken curries and used in vegetable patties.

Tamarind Concentrate: Extract of sour tasting tropical fruit which looks like broad bean. Concentrate is reddish black in colour and stays well in fridge for a year. Lemon juice can be substituted for tamarind if it is not on hand but the curry will be of lighter colour.

Turmeric: Yellow powder made from rhizome is used in almost all indian preparations, its yellow colour gives distinct colour to curries. Turmeric has preservative property hence it is always used in pickles.

Tofu: This is made from soya bean and is available in supermarkets or continental shops, it looks like a square block of creamy soft cheese. When opened, refrigerate in fresh water and daily change water. It has no fat and is very high in protein.

Udad Daal: skinned and split black udad, daal is white in colour and oval in shape. This is the lentil used in papadams and lentil patties. It is very popular in southern India.

Yellow Colour: Edible yellow colouring available in powder form or as liquid and is available in all supermarkets, commonly used to colour cakes.